ORANGEVI
3 0610

Discarded
from the
Library

FUN FACE PAINTING IDEAS FOR KIDS

NICK & BRIAN **WOLFE**

CINCINNATI, OHIO
WWW.IMPACT-BOOKS.COM **IMPACT**

D0905546

CONTENTS

Orangeville Public Library
I Mill Street
Orangeville, ON L9W 2M2

(519) 941-0610

INTRODUCTION

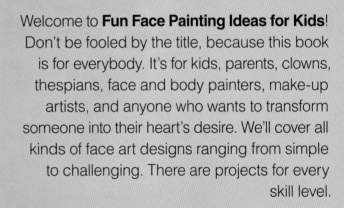

Welcome to **Fun Face Painting Ideas for Kids**! Don't be fooled by the title, because this book is for everybody. It's for kids, parents, clowns, thespians, face and body painters, make-up artists, and anyone who wants to transform someone into their heart's desire. We'll cover all kinds of face art designs ranging from simple to challenging. There are projects for every skill level.

With this book, we hope to raise public awareness of this form of art. It truly is for everyone. We all have faces, don't we? Face art does not discriminate. Anyone can paint a face or have their own face painted.

We also hope that this book will always remain with you and continue to provide inspiration while you grow as an artist. This book was designed to be shared so be sure to show people your favorite face art designs from these pages, as well as your own original creations that they inspire.

Materials

You don't need a ton of stuff to get started painting faces. Brushes and paints are the essentials.

PAINTS

Use water-based theatrical makeup that is hypo allergenic and nontoxic. Acrylic paint is not made for face painting and should be avoided. Every brand of face paint works. Some have more pigment and brighter colors, while some are easier to wash off. Decide which characteristic is more important to you and go with that.

BRUSHES

We use small synthetic rounds. Make sure they have stiff bristles with sharp points that can yield a fine line.

Stick with a no. 3 round for ideal control. The bigger the brush size, the less control you'll have, which means the lighter your touch will need to be. A no. 3 round allows you to make a really thin line. By applying more pressure, you can produce a wide line as well.

If you find your linework is a bit heavy-handed, try a no. 1 round. Use a no. 6 round for very wide lines. A filbert brush is a good choice for dragging and blending color because of its rounded head and very thick bristles. All these brushes can be found in any art or craft store.

OTHER MATERIALS

Cotton swabs cut in half are useful as disposable applicators, erasers (when used with a little water) or disposable brushes. You'll also need sponges. We recommend firm sponges with rounded edges and large pores. The sponges used for this book are pottery sponges cut in half. Hand sanitizer, baby wipes and loose polyester glitter are also great items for your kit.

FACE PAINTING KIT SETUP

All face painting kits are unique, but this is our typical setup. One color per sponge is recommended. Use one end for the paint and keep one end dry for blending.

SPLIT PAINT CAKES

Split cakes have both the dark and light shades of a color. Some have one half UV-reactive (black light) paint. The idea is to have more color choices in a smaller kit and to be able to mix colors to achieve maximum coverage and the brightest color. Colors can be mixed right on top of the cake as well. Wipe the cake clean with a baby wipe to get it back to the original condition.

USING SPONGES

Wet only the very tip of the sponge. The amount of water determines how much paint there will be to work with. If you wipe a sponge across the cake a few times, the makeup will be thin, watery and transparent. Rub the sponge many times and the makeup becomes thick and opaque.

COLOR WHEEL

Make yourself a simple color wheel to help you choose colors. Colors on the same side of the color wheel blend easily—for instance, yellow, orange and red. Yellow is often used to highlight because it is brighter. To paint a green ball, for example, use blue for shade and yellow to highlight.

Another way to change the value of the base color is to add black (for shade) or white (for highlight). You can also create highlights by adding white to an adjacent color on the wheel. For example, to highlight purple, use light blue or light red.

Paint Allergies

Rarely is anyone allergic to face paint. Allergies will usually result in discomfort within a minute or so of application. If this happens, wash off the paint with soap and warm water and discontinue use. We have painted hundreds of thousands of faces from all over the world and have never witnessed a reaction, but it could happen.

Sponge Techniques

The sponge is used to cover the face quickly with thin amounts of paint. Twisting the sponge in different directions can really add detail. Always test a sponge first to see how wet the paint is that's on it. It may have plenty of paint and water from the last face you painted. The sponge is a very versatile tool, so don't be afraid to use it a lot. Practice and pay attention to what you do and what the results are.

Stippling

This is one of the most useful sponge techniques. Stippling is great for blending color, suggesting texture, indicating highlights and suggesting facial hair. To get the most realistic result, hold your half sponge upside down so the rounded part touches the skin. Using the edge of the sponge would result in lines—something you want to avoid when stippling.

Circular Strokes

Circular strokes can be used for cheek art and sectioning off parts of the face. A rounded sponge is perfect for this. The sponging doesn't have to be perfect; just try to make it as close as possible. The edges can be corrected with a brush later.

Fur Technique

Use the fur technique to create striation patterns not only for fur textures, but also for muscle patterns and creature textures. If executed correctly, you can create a lot of detail quickly.

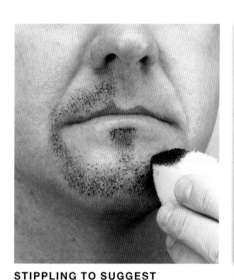

STIPPLING TO SUGGEST FACIAL HAIR

Lightly tap the sponge in an even pattern.

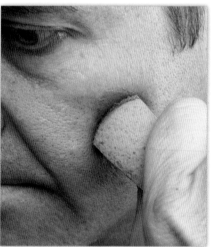

MAKING CIRCULAR STROKES

To make a circular stroke with your sponge, simply apply the end of the sponge to the face and spin.

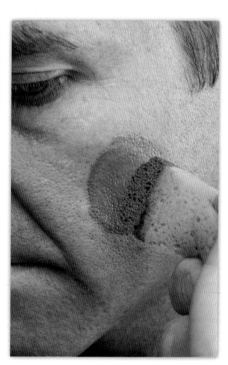

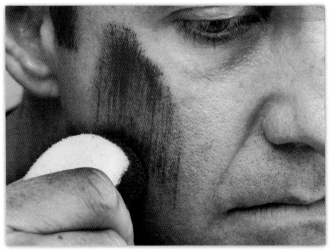

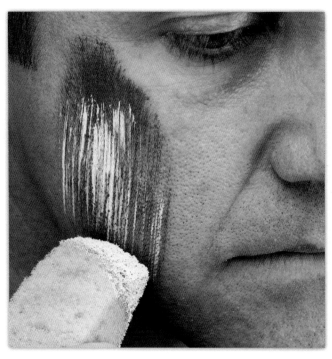

CREATING FUR

Fill your sponge with paint, then pull it in a downward motion across the face. Then, go back in with a second color, lightly dragging your sponge over the basecoat to indicate more texture.

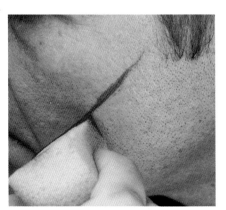

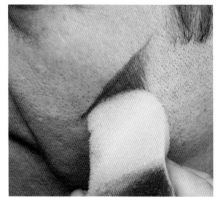

PAINTING LINE STROKES

Use the edge of your sponge to place line strokes.

DRAGGING COLOR

Pull color by dragging with the end of your sponge out from the paint.

BLENDING COLOR

Blend colors with the clean end of your sponge.

ADDING DOTS

Make dots with the corner of your sponge.

Brush Techniques

When painting lines, pretend your brush is dancing. The more fluid and confident your brushstrokes are, the more pleasing the design will be. Practice your linework often. Use your arm or thigh to warm up on and try new techniques. Hold the brush like a pencil and close to the end for more control. Sometimes, it helps to use your pinky finger to steady your hand. Nice linework can really save sloppy sponge work.

Remember, he who paints most, paints best. To become a quick and accurate painter, practice and focus!

Painting Thin to Thick to Thin Lines
Using this type of line gives your face paintings style and depth, not to mention they will look fancier.

Painting Stars
Add stars to your face paintings to give you extra flare or excitement. Whether painting a five-pointed star or a starburst, creating the perfect shape is all in the wrist. Simply flick your brush lightly, stroke by stroke, to create any star shape you desire.

1 Begin Thin to Thick
Begin the brushstroke before your brush meets the skin. Then, gently touch the tip of your brush to the face, gradually applying more pressure toward mid-stroke.

2 Finish Thick to Thin
Once the thickest part of the line has been laid in, slowly begin picking your brush up off the skin as you move toward the end of the stroke.

 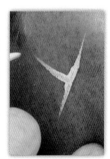   

1 Begin the Star
Place your brush on what will be the center point of the star and flick a line down.

2 Add the Second Stroke
Flick your brush to the left.

3 Place the Third Stroke
Next, flick your brush to the right to form a cross.

4 Develop the Star
Fill in your star with more small flicks radiating from the center.

THE FINISHED RESULT
By beginning in the center and working out, your stars will look as though they are bursting and exploding with energy.

Painting Swirls and Curls

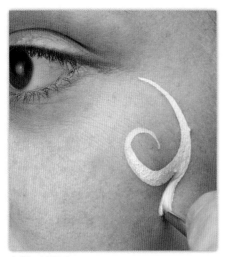

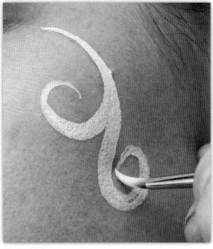

1 Start Thick
Press your brush down toward the face when drawing the thickest part of your swirl or curl.

2 Go Thin
Conversely, apply barely any pressure at all when drawing the thinnest part.

How to Remove Paint

To remove face paint, use any of these items:

- COLD CREAM
- LOTION
- BABY SHAMPOO
- BABY OIL
- BABY WIPES

Massage any of these into the face, then wipe it off immediately. Use eye makeup remover to get off any paint placed around the eyes.

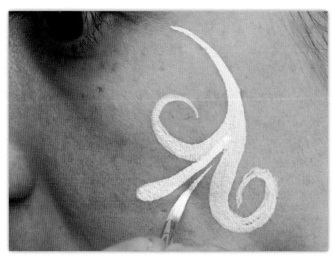

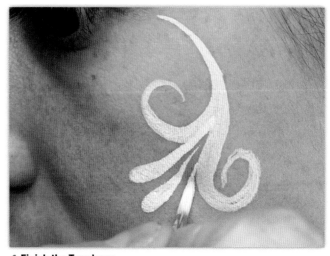

3 Begin Adding Teardrop Shapes
Create the thin point of the drop, applying light pressure with the tip of your brush.

4 Finish the Teardrops
Gradually increase pressure and flatten the brush as you move toward the thicker end of the drop.

Painting Flames

Fire is timeless. It inspires passion. Whether you paint a flaming soccer ball or a fire-breathing dragon, flames are always a hot design. The key to painting fire is to keep the top of the flames pointy and the bottom of the flames curvy. This takes time to perfect, so just keep practicing.

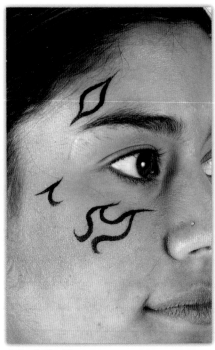

1 Begin the Flames
There are three basic shapes used to create fire designs—a blimp or eye shape, a crested wave shape, and a thin-to-thick-to-thin horse-shoe shape.

2 Build Up the Flames
Link the individual flame shapes together with scoops.

3 Color the Flames
Fill in the flames with red, yellow and orange. It is your choice whether to apply the colored paint with a brush, or to stipple it on with a sponge. So long as the shape and color of flames is there, it will translate as fire.

Painting Feathers

Feathers work well for adding detail to many kinds of face paint designs such as Native American themes, Mardi Gras masks, angels and birds. There are many different ways to paint feathers. Let's explore one of them.

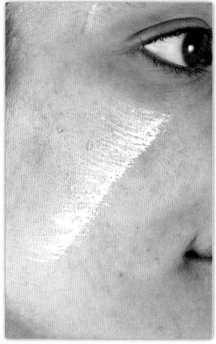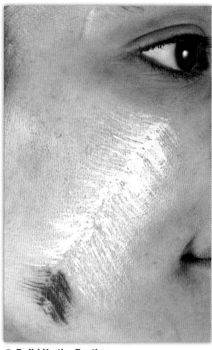

1 Begin the Feather
Load the tip of a sponge with white and a tiny bit of water—just a drop or two. Run it down the cheek in a straight line while flicking out.

2 Build Up the Feather
Flick white in the opposite direction to create the other side of the feather.

3 Define the Feather
Use black to outline the feather and paint in the spine. Highlight with more white. Sharpen the feather tip with red.

Painting Eyes

The design of the eyes is the most important part of the look of the characters you paint. Is your dragon supposed to be scary or cute? It all depends on the eyes. They are what everyone will look at first.

Your hand or arm is a good place to practice your painting.

1 Begin a Cute Eye
Draw a small arch to indicate the cheek. Place a larger arch above the small one to suggest the eye. Connect the end to the small arch.

2 Build Up
Add a thick half arch inside the eye for the iris.

3 Add Eyelashes
Add three thick-to-thin strokes at the corner of the eye to lay in the eyelashes.

4 Finish With Highlights
Add white highlights to the cheek and the whites of the eye.

1 Begin a Mean Eye
Paint a sideways S shape for the eyebrow.

2 Build Up
Add an almond-shaped eye beneath the brow.

3 Shade the Eyebrow
Add shadows beneath the brow and the eye.

4 Finish With White
Fill in the eye with white.

Cotton Swab Techniques

Inexpensive and disposable, cotton swabs are an invaluable tool to have around.

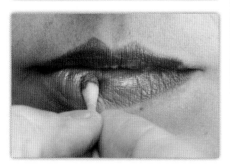

APPLYING PAINT TO LIPS
Using a cotton swab on lips is less ticklish and gives the artist a more sanitary approach than using a brush. After the lips are painted, you can throw away the swab.

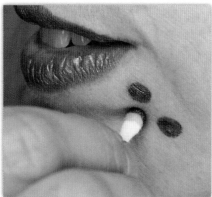

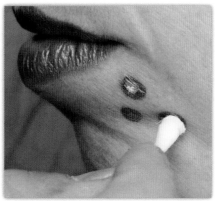

LAYING IN DOTS
Dots made with a swab tend to be more consistent. If you need your dots to be the same size (like the rivets on a helmet), definitely use a cotton swab.

ERASING MISTAKES
There really isn't any erasing in face painting. "Mistakes" are integrated into the design—using glitter for girls and blood for boys. If you need to clean up edges or lift out some color, dip a cotton swab in water and apply it to the spot. To clean up drips, however, wipe the skin with a moist towelette or tissue.

Cuts and Blemishes

If a model has any cuts or blemishes, use a cotton swab to paint around the wound without contaminating your brush or sponges. Bad sunburn, eczema, chicken pox sores and cold sores, etc. should always be avoided as the makeup may irritate the skin further.

More Important Techniques

Here are a few more techniques good to have in your repertoire as you begin painting faces.

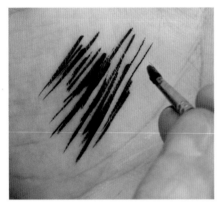

CREATING FUR TEXTURE

To suggest fur using your brush, flick the brush back and forth using the thin to thick to thin line technique. Paint in short, quick strokes for the best results. This is the technique used for moustaches, beards and animal fur.

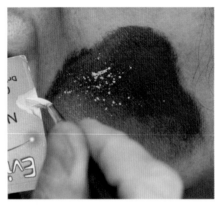

SPATTERING

Spattering can be used for texture on rocks, for stars in outer space, as freckles, or as blood spraying from a wound. Using your brush, flick paint from a card aimed at the area you want to spatter.

MOTTLING

Mottling is painting random squiggles and dots to break up a smooth paint job and make something appear more textured. We use this a lot with zombie skin and monsters. It adds dimension and detail. Use the side of your brush to add wiggly strokes for mottling in texture. The brush shouldn't be too wet and the paint should be thinned.

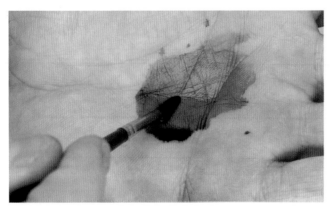

APPLYING A WASH

Place a dab of paint in your palm, then water it down to create a thin consistency. Washes work well for shadowing beneath objects, making them pop off the face.

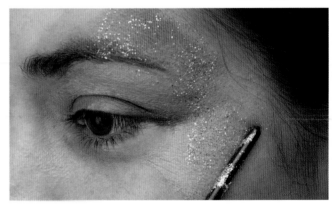

APPLYING GLITTER

Dip the end of a round brush in glitter and roll it onto wet paint.

Shading and Outlining

Shading and outlining are the basic painting skills that are good to master as you paint the projects. Practice with a simple sphere.

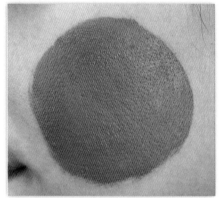

1 Establish the Basic Shape
Apply a basecoat in the shape of the object you wish to portray.

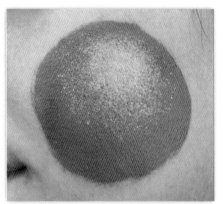

2 Add Highlight for Dimension
Apply the highlight thickly in one small spot. Then stipple the color out from the bright center, overlapping the highlight.

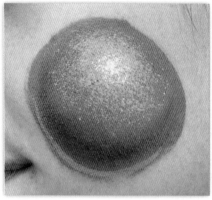

3 Place Shadows and Highlights
Apply a darker shade toward the bottom of the sphere, leaving a little line of the midtone to represent reflected color. Then, apply white to the very center of the yellow highlight, and add a white highlight on the reflected color at the bottom of the sphere.

4 Outline the Shape
Outline the sphere using a brush. When outlining, don't look at the tip of your brush. Rather, look at the object you are outlining and let your eye trace the outside. Your brush will automatically follow your eye.

When you finish a stroke but need to keep the outline going, don't start a new stroke at the end of the finished stroke. Instead, overlap the strokes so the line is consistent.

Adding a dark shadow underneath the sphere makes it appear to be resting on a surface.

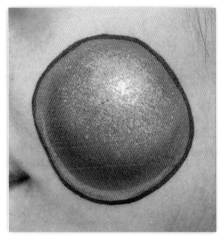

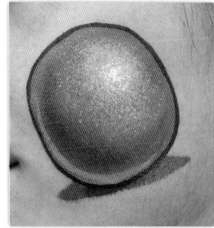

FUN **FACES**

Cute, funny or scary—all the faces we paint are fun faces. Our most important rule in face art is to have fun. Whether we're painting pretty butterflies or scary monsters, we're having fun and making sure that everyone else is too. Even at times when a design doesn't turn out the way we planned, we still consider it a win so long as everybody had fun.

The following demos will take you, step by step, through creating some of our funniest, silliest and scariest face painting designs yet. You can copy them exactly as they are, or use them as inspiration for creating your own unique face art. It's up to you—just have fun!

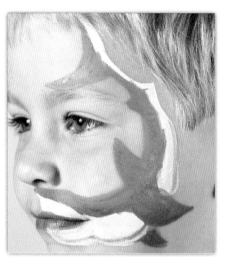

1 Use white and a no. 3 round brush to paint the shark's underbelly along the temple and side of the face. Paint the lower portion of the shark's face across the mouth and jawline. Continue using the no. 3 round brush for the remaining steps.

2 Paint in the rest of the shark's body and fins with gray. Add a slight gray shadow line to the underbelly.

3 Outline the shark's body and paint in the eye and nostril in black.

4 Paint the teeth and add highlights along the head, fins and tail with white. Paint in the gills with black.

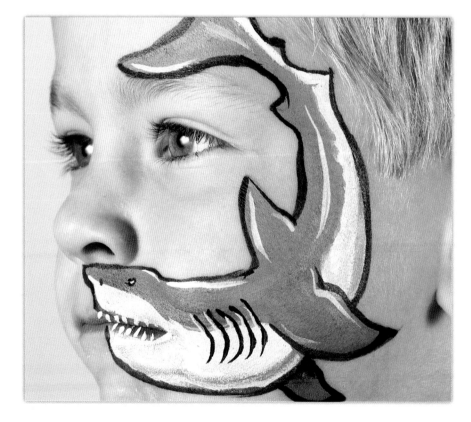

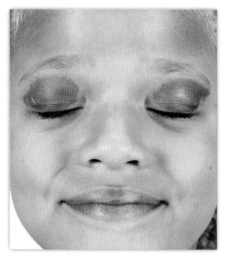 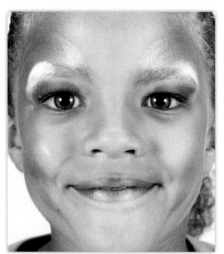 

1 Use a sponge to apply pink and purple across the eyelids.

2 Sponge white highlights onto the ends of the eyebrows. Sponge gold in the shape of angel wings, arching upward from the eyebrows and continuing down the cheeks.

3 Using a no. 3 round brush and gold, paint a halo in the center of the forehead. Outline the feathers in white. Continue using the no. 3 round brush for the remaining steps.

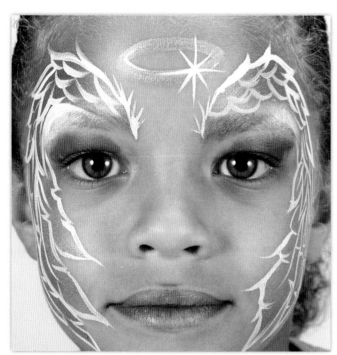 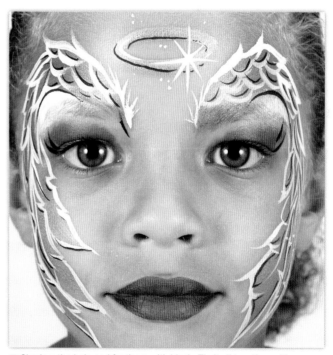

4 Highlight the halo and scallop the feathers at the top of the wings with white.

5 Shadow the halo and feathers with black. Tie it all together with purple lipstick.

1 Sponge a gray basecoat onto the face and ears. Leave a blank area around the parameter of the face.

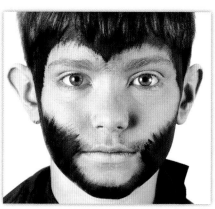

2 Sponge black along the edge of the face, gently dragging in toward the center. This will give the effect of fur.

3 Use a sponge to shade black around the eyes. Then switch to a no. 3 round brush and drag more black in from the edges of the face to further enhance the fur effect. Continue using the same brush for the remaining steps.

4 Paint in the nose and outline the eyebrow with black.

5 Paint crow's feet and wrinkles around the eyes. Lightly stipple white onto the cheeks, nose and lips to add highlights. Use your fingers to paint in highlights around the crow's feet.

1 Mix a bit of brown into orange. Sponge the basic shape of the owl over and around the eyes.

2 Paint the owl's face with white using a no. 3 round brush. Begin painting feathers on the upper areas of the wings using the tear-drop technique. Continue using the no. 3 round brush for the remaining steps.

DOWNLOAD A FREE BONUS DEMO AT **IMPACT-BOOKS.COM/WOLFEBROTHERS**

3 Paint white lines across the ridge of the eyes. Use the tear-drop technique to add feathers to the tail and lower areas of the wings.

4 Continuing with white, build up the feathers using the scalloping technique.

5 Line the eyelids and outline the mask in black. Add points at the ends of the feather tips.

CREATE A NATURAL LOOK

Work quickly when painting the scallops. This will give them a natural-looking variation. Use the very tip of a round brush to achieve the thinnest lines.

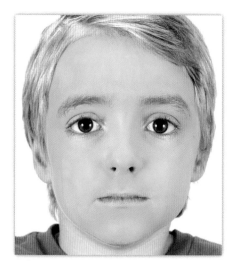

1 Sponge a lime green basecoat over the entire face.

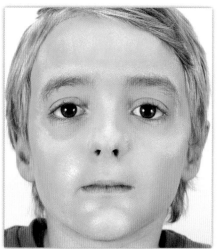

2 Stipple in yellow highlights with a sponge, covering the areas at the tops of the cheeks, nose, chin and forehead.

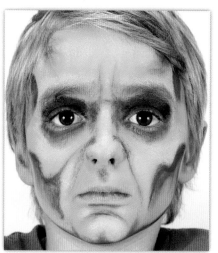

3 Use dark green and a sponge to shadow around the eyes, temples, cheekbones, jawline and chin.

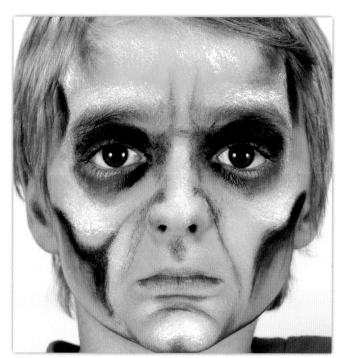

4 Sponge black over the dark green to darken the shadows. Use a sponge dipped in a bit of white to highlight the yellow areas.

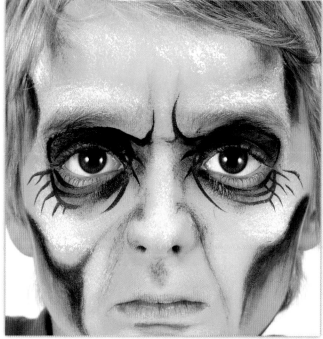

5 Paint in crow's feet, wrinkles and bags under the eyes using black and a no. 3 round brush.

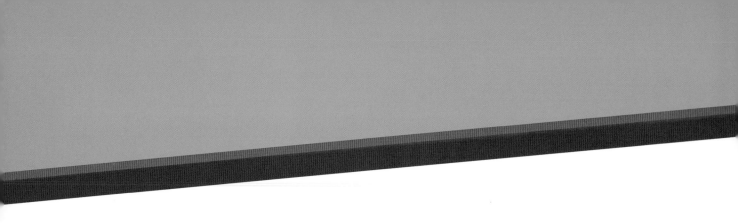

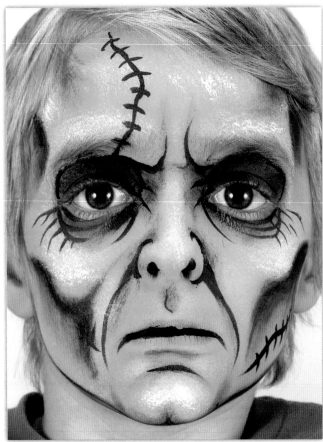

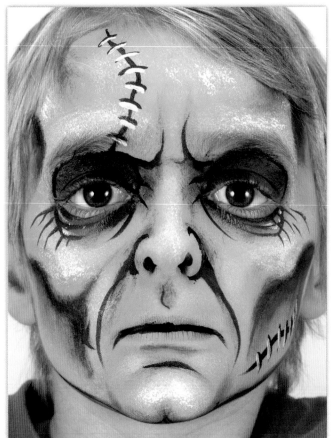

6 Continue with the same color and brush. Add cuts, stitches and any other details you like.

7 Highlight the stitches with white to finish.

KEEP IT SUBTLE AND DON'T RUSH
Make sure that the scar and black stitches are completely dry before you begin adding the white highlights.

In the close-up shot below, you can see that the stippled highlight has not been blended in all the way. Try to keep the layers subtle as you mix them on the face.

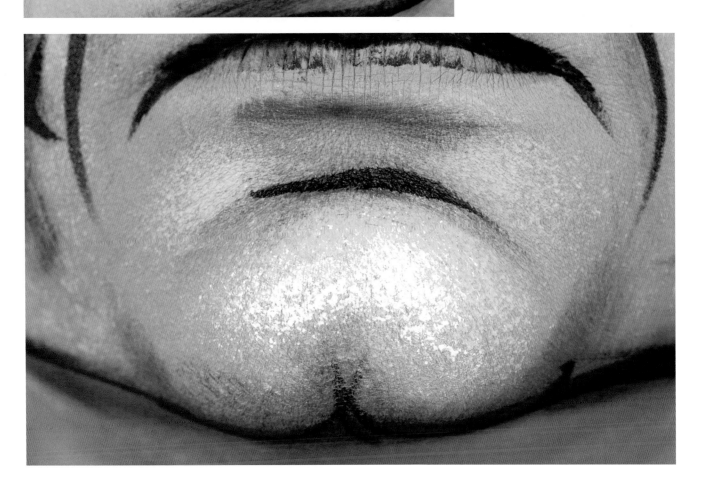

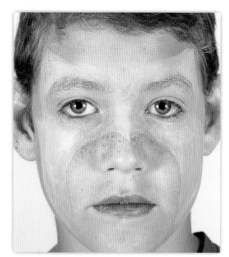

1 Sponge a yellow basecoat onto the face in the shape of a mask.

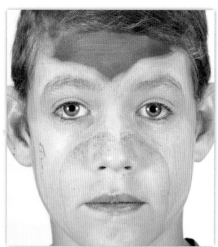

2 Double load a sponge with blue and apply a triangle shape above the mask.

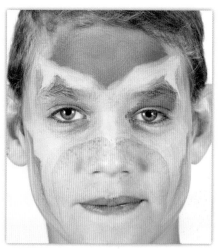

3 Using a sponge and orange, shade in the eyes, temples and cheeks.

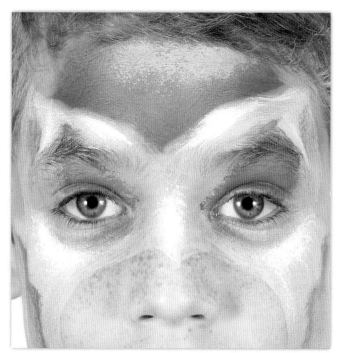

4 Sponge in white highlights across the cheekbones, eyebrows and bridge of the nose. Sponge in light blue highlights at the very top of the blue triangle shape.

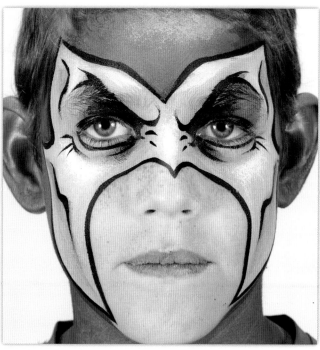

5 Add wrinkles and outline the mask using a no. 3 round brush and black. Usc a sponge to shade the eyes with black as well. Sponge blue across the neck and ears.

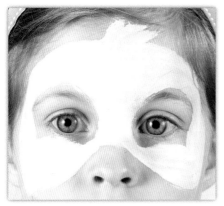

1 Apply a white basecoat to the top half of the face using a sponge. Drag the sponge upward to suggest feathers at the top of the forehead.

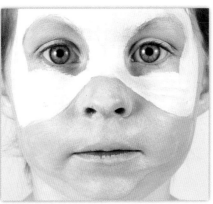

2 Sponge yellow onto the bottom half of the face to create the beak. Sponge light blue above the eyes.

3 Use a no. 3 round brush to outline the eyes and top of the head with dark blue.

4 Continuing with the no. 3 round brush, outline the beak and add nostrils and eyelashes with black.

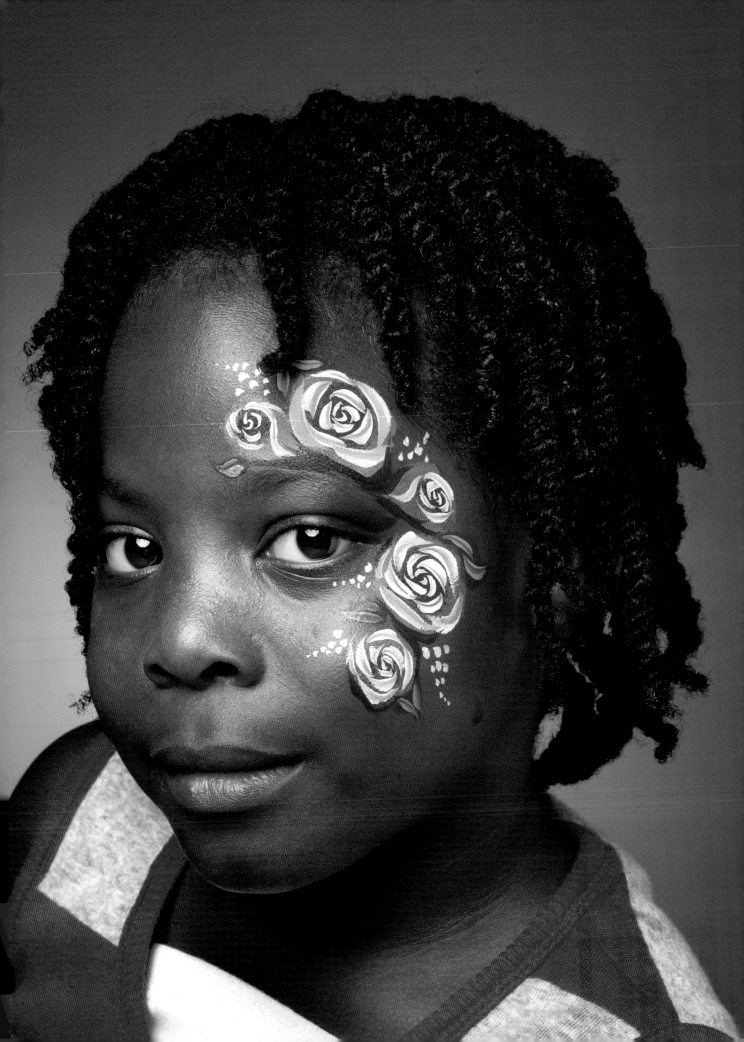

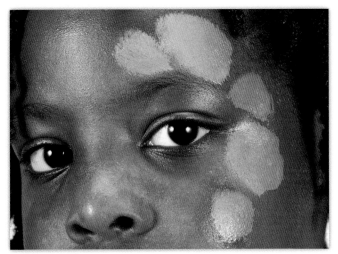

1 Sponge pink circular shapes above the eyebrow and along the temple and cheekbone.

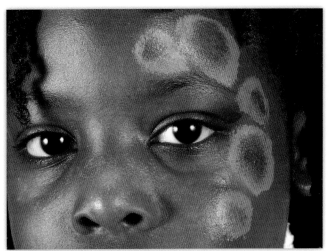

2 Stipple red into the middle of the circles with a sponge. Shade above the eyes with a bit of red as well.

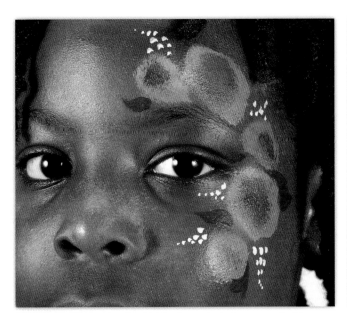

3 With a no. 3 round brush, paint the leaves in dark green and add some small white dots to suggest baby's breath. Continue using the no. 3 round brush for the remaining steps.

4 Paint white highlights into the roses. Start small in the center, gradually spiralling out into larger strokes as you move closer to the edge of each flower.

5 Continue using white and the scalloping technique to finish highlighting the roses. Paint light green highlights into the leaves.

6 Shade under and around the roses with red to finish.

ADD DIMENSION

Pressing harder on the brush while painting the petals will push the paint toward the outer edges of the brushstroke. This will help add dimension to the rose petals.

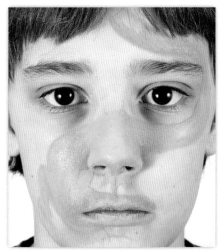

1 Using a sponge, apply a green basecoat onto the face in the shape of a crocodile.

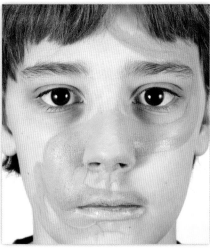

2 With the tips of your fingers, paint yellow highlights onto the crocodile's underbelly, neck and bottom jaw.

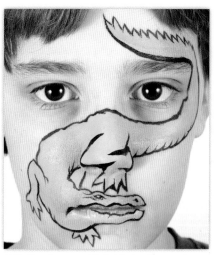

3 Outline the crocodile in black with a no. 2 round brush.

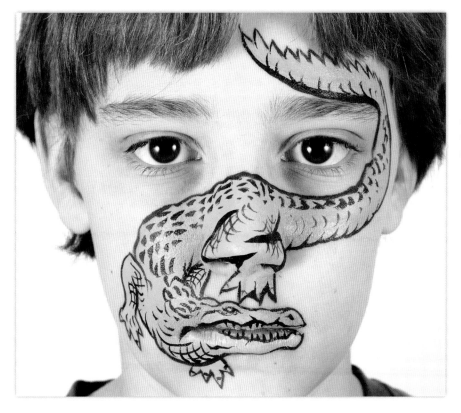

4 Continuing with the no. 2 round brush, use crosshatching to paint in scales along the back and limbs in black.

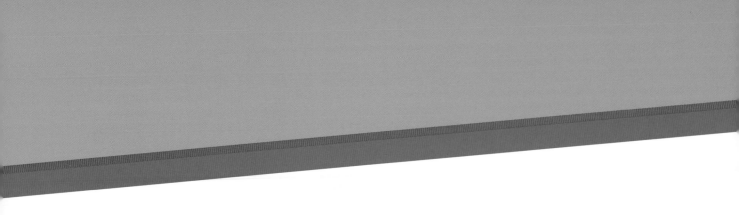

5 Paint the teeth, toenails and eyes in white with the no. 2 round brush. Add black stripes along the back for heightened detail with the side of a round brush.

6 Create a watered-down mixture of black and brown paint in the palm of your hand. Continue adding water until the mixture is translucent. With the no. 2 round brush, paint a shadow below the crocodile. Be sure to leave a greater distance between the shadow and the head and tail—this will give it the illusion of being 3-D.

REALISTIC EYES

Crocodiles have tiny eyes in proportion to the size of their heads, so keep your croc's eyes tiny if you want him to look realistic. Paint larger eyes only if you're going for a cute or cartoon look.

USE THE SIDE OF YOUR BRUSH FOR THICK LINES

The stripes on the tail were created with the side of a round brush.

1 Sponge a white basecoat in the shape of a pony's profile across the eye and down the cheek. Sponge in the mane running down the nose, mouth and chin in light blue.

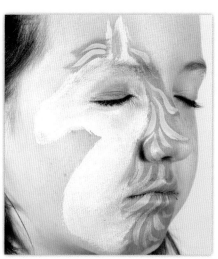

2 Use a sponge to shadow the eye, ears and nose in pink. Paint highlights into the mane with white and a no. 3 round brush.

3 Continue with the no. 3 round brush and paint gray spots of various sizes on the pony's face and neck. Sponge black onto the eyelid for shadowing. Switch back to a no. 3 round to paint the pony's eyelashes in the corner of the eye with black.

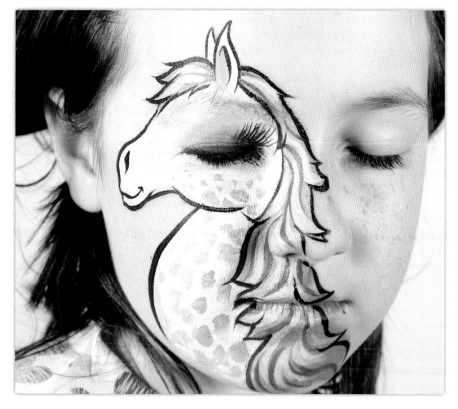

4 Continue using the same brush and color to paint in the pony's mouth and nose. Build up the white highlights in the mane and add in some dark blue low lights as well. Paint some extra eyelashes under the eyelid in black.

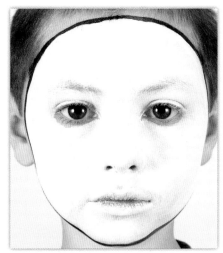

1 Sponge the entire face with white and then outline with black using a no. 3 round brush.

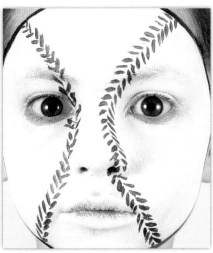

2 Continuing with the no. 3 round brush, add red stitches in a V-pattern running down the right and left sides of the face. Paint the stitches so that each side runs in an opposite direction.

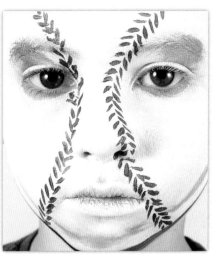

3 Sponge gray above the eyelids, around the chin and onto one side of the jawline to create shadows.

4 Using black and a no. 3 round brush, paint in "mean" eyebrows, wrinkles and crow's feet.

5 Paint in the mouth, teeth and cheeks in black with the same brush.

1 Use a no. 3 round brush and dark blue to paint the bat's head and body, leaving two blank oval shapes where the eyes will be. Continue using the no. 3 round brush for the remaining steps.

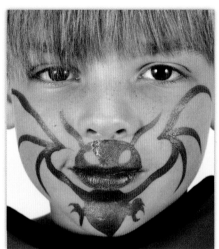

2 Paint in the bat's legs, feet and wings in dark blue.

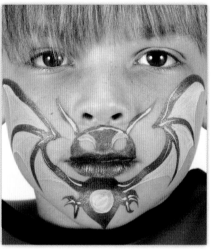

3 Paint the inside of the wings and highlight the bat's feet, stomach, face and ears with light blue.

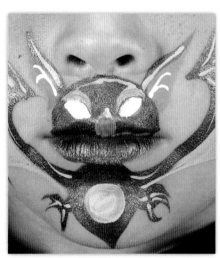

4 Paint the eyes white. Use pink for the nose and inside of the ears. Then highlight the ears with white.

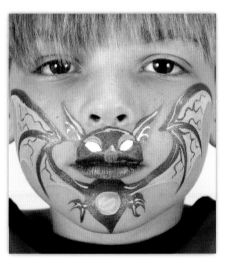

5 Mix blue and pink to make purple. Paint purple veins onto the wings. Use this same color to shadow the ears as well.

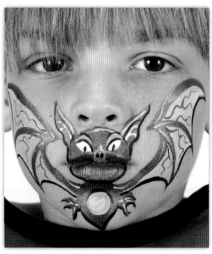

6 Outline the bat's body and add shadows under the wings with black.

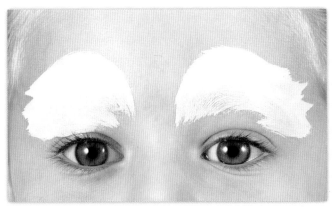

1 Sponge white in the basic shape of a swan's body above each eyebrow.

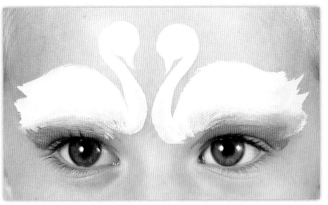

2 Sponge pink onto the eyelids. Paint the swans' heads and necks with white and a no. 3 round brush. Continue using the no. 3 round brush for the remaining steps.

3 Paint white swirls, curls, tear drops and dots around the corners of the eyes and on the cheeks. Add two black teardrop shapes onto the front of the swans' faces.

4 Paint the swans' beaks yellow. Outline the swans and swirls with purple. Paint purple over the eyebrows. Finish with pink lipstick.

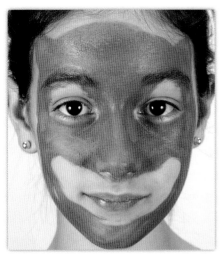

1 Sponge on a pink basecoat covering most of the face, with two pointed ears at the top. Leave the areas around the eyes and mouth blank.

2 Sponge yellow onto the eyelids, extending up to the eyebrows. Sponge white onto the ears, cheeks and mouth.

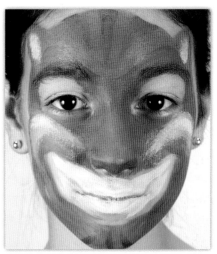

3 Mix pink and blue to get purple. With a no. 3 round brush, paint the tip of the nose purple and add purple stripes onto the forehead and chin.

4 Continuing with the same brush, paint the teeth and outline the mouth with dark brown.

5 Use a sponge to lightly shade dark green at the top of the eyes, then sponge white onto the bottom of the eyes. Outline the eyes and add eyelashes with black and a no. 3 round brush.

6 Continuing with the same color and brush, outline the face, define the eyelashes, and add pupils and whisker dots. Fill in the gums with pink and add white highlights.

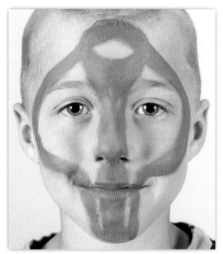

1 Use a sponge to apply an orange basecoat onto the face in the shape of a hissing cobra.

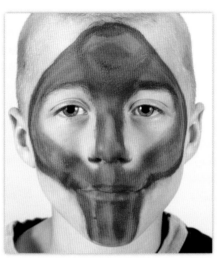

2 Sponge red around both the inside and outside of the orange basecoat.

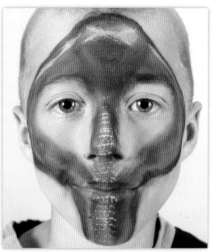

3 Sponge yellow around the eyes and upper cheeks. Stipple yellow highlights running down the nose, lips and chin.

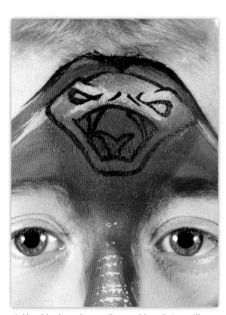

4 Use black and a no. 3 round brush to outline the basic shape of the cobra's face. Then paint in the eyes and mouth.

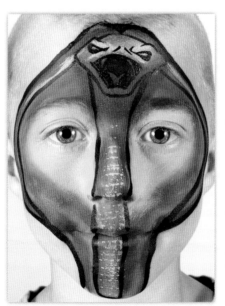

5 Continuing with the same brush and color, outline the rest of the cobra's body and darken the mouth.

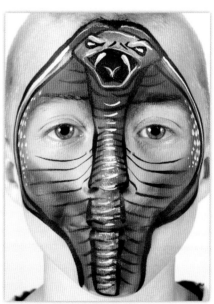

6 Add bands of black to further detail the body. Use white to paint the eyes, teeth and additional highlights.

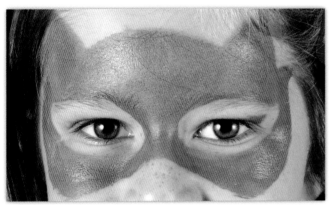

1 Sponge pink in the shape of a cat mask across the eyes, cheeks and forehead. Mix pink and blue to get purple. Sponge purple onto the eyelids as eyeshadow.

2 Outline the mask using black and a no. 3 round brush. Use a sponge to blend white highlights into the eyeshadow.

4 Paint the inside of the ears using black and a no. 3 round brush. Use the side of the same brush to paint loose *C* shapes for the cheetah pattern.

5 Finish the main shapes of the cheetah pattern, then add several small black dots across the pattern. Tie it all together with purple lipstick.

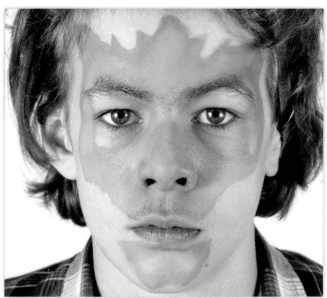

1 Sponge a basecoat of light green on the forehead in a spiked pattern. Continue sponging the basecoat around the eyes, nose, cheekbones and chin.

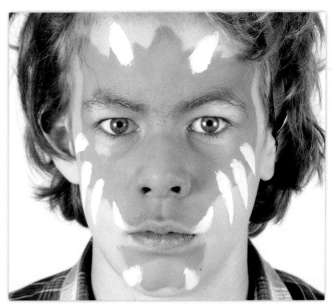

2 Use the edge of a sponge to paint the horns in white.

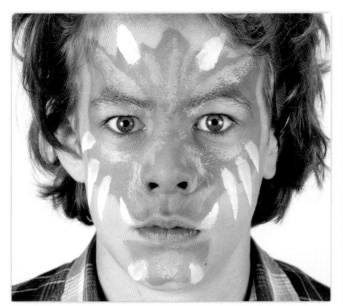

3 Stipple yellow highlights onto the face with the tip of a sponge.

4 Sponge dark green shadows around the eyes, nose, and at the bottom of the chin to add some depth.

5 Sponge black over the eyes to create more shadowing. Stipple white highlights over the yellow areas.

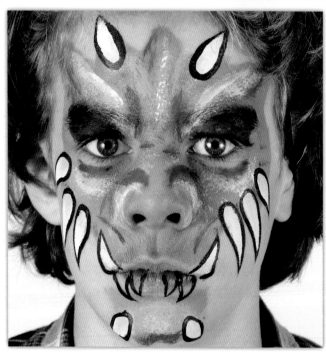

6 Outline the horns and paint the teeth using black and a no. 3 round brush. Continue using the no. 3 round brush for the remaining steps.

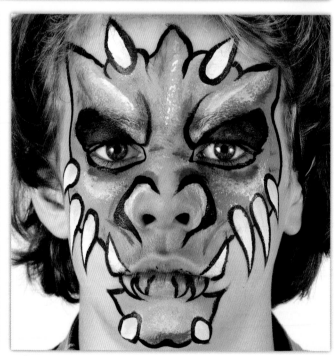

7 Outline the nose, eyes and rest of the face in black.

8 Continue with black to paint in eyebrows, crow's feet and elongate the nostrils.

9 Add white highlights. Detail the horns and lips with red.

1 Mix dark blue with pink to get a purple shade. Sponge the basic shape of the elephant's head onto the forehead. Sponge the shape for the elephant's trunk running down the nose, lips and chin. Add a bit of pink onto the very end of the trunk.

2 Add a little more blue to your paint mixture to get a darker purple shade. Sponge this onto the forehead, cheeks, and around the eyes, following the basic shape of elephant ears/butterfly wings.

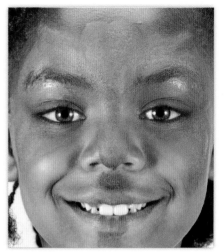

3 Stipple in pink highlights with a sponge.

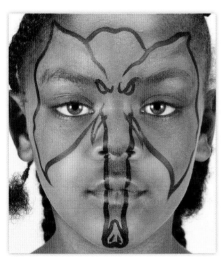

4 Outline with black using a no. 3 round brush. Paint in the eyes, tusks and nostrils.

5 Continuing with the same brush and color, pattern the elephant ears/butterfly wings. Add eyebrows and antennae to the elephant's face.

6 Paint in white teardrops and dots to highlight the ears/wings. Paint the eyes green, then highlight the eyes and antennae with yellow. Apply black eyeliner to tie it all together.

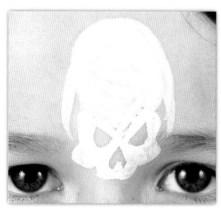

1 Paint the upper part of the spider's face on the forehead and between the eyebrows with white and a no. 3 round brush. Continue using the no. 3 round brush for the remaining steps.

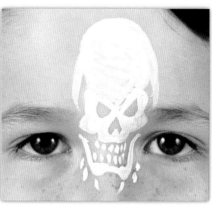

2 Paint in the lower part of the spider's face on the bridge of the nose and between the eyes.

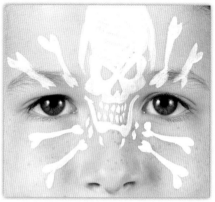

3 Begin painting the bone segments extending out from the nose and above the eyes. Use the tear-drop technique for the ends of the bones.

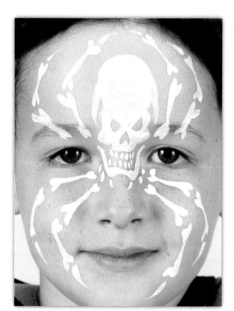

4 Finish painting the remaining bone segments on the forehead and extending down the cheeks.

5 Outline the spider's face and fill in the eyes and nose with black. Paint a red hourglass shape on the spider's head.

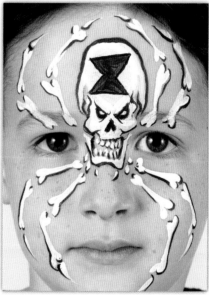

6 Continue using black to outline the hourglass and shadow the bones. Dot the eyes with white.

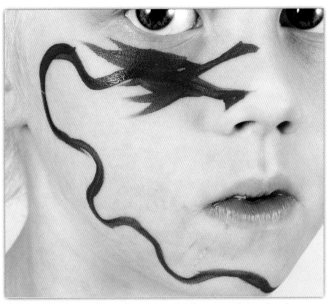

1 Use red and a no. 3 round brush to paint the wyvern's head and an action line for where the body and tail will be. Continue with the same brush for the remaining steps.

2 Paint the frame of the wings and feet in red.

3 Use pink to paint the inside of the wyvern's mouth and wings.

4 Paint yellow onto the wing tips and horns, and add yellow scales to the belly.

5 Paint in teeth and highlight the wings and body with white.

6 Outline the wyvern's body, tail and underside of the wings in black.

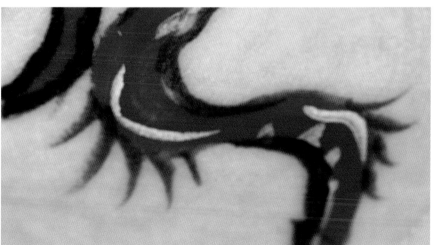

EXPERIMENT!

Have fun experimenting with different colors and maybe adding more details like fire. Basically, so long as your wyvern has a mean eye and lots of teeth and spikes, everybody will love it!

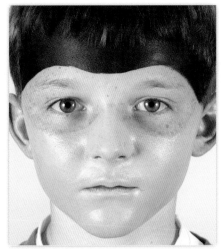

1 Sponge a basecoat of black onto the forehead and yellow onto the middle and lower sections of the face. Leave the area around the eyes clear.

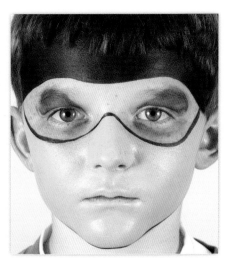

2 Sponge a bit of brown above and under the eyes to create shadowing. Outline the mask with black and a no. 3 round brush.

3 Continue using black and the no. 3 round brush to paint in eyebrows. Paint four M-shapes in descending size down the front of the face. This will help to camouflage the facial features.

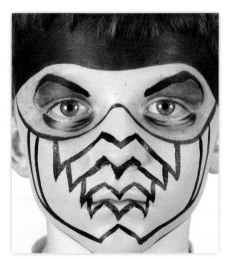

4 Still using the no. 3 round brush, add bags under the eyes with dark brown. Connect the Ms into more detailed lines and patterns following the contours of the facial anatomy.

5 Continue adding more details to the mask and paint wrinkles on the forehead and around the eyes with black and a no. 3 round brush.

6 Use a filbert brush to drag some of the black paint into the yellow areas between the lines. Paint in white highlights with a no. 3 round brush. Sponge black onto the ears.

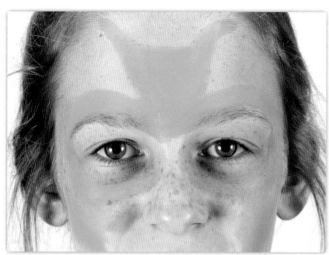

1 Sponge a basecoat of lime green onto the forehead and cheeks and around the eyes in the shape shown here. This will form the base for the frog's head and legs.

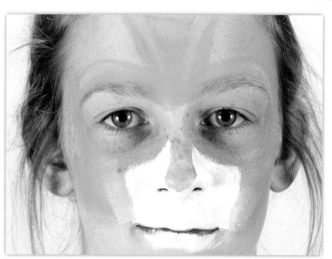

2 Sponge white over the mouth, inner cheeks and sides of the nose. This will form the frog's belly. Sponge yellow highlights onto the forehead and around the green on the inner cheeks.

3 Sponge red onto the forehead in two large teardrop shapes to make the frog's eyes. Continue sponging red around the eyes and down the center of the nose to form the frog's mouth. Sponge orange along both sides of the chin for the feet.

4 Paint the toes in yellow using a cotton swab. Twist the swab as you apply the paint to get a good circle shape. Use a no. 3 round brush to sharpen up the red areas. Continue with the same brush for the remaining steps.

5 Outline the head and mouth and paint in the pupils with black.

6 Continue outlining the legs and feet with black.

7 Add white highlights to the head, eyes, mouth legs and toes. Paint a fly onto the tip of the frog's tongue, using black for the body, white for the wings, and blue for the eyes.

DETAIL POSSIBILITIES ARE ENDLESS

Instead of a fly, you might want to try a ladybug or dragonfly to switch things up a bit. Why not? Just have fun with it!

FROM A DISTANCE

Notice the toe highlights are not blended in. This effect looks good from a few feet away.

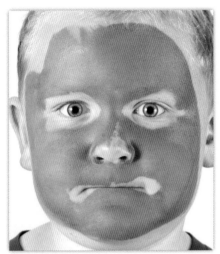

1 Sponge a basecoat of orange over the entire face. Don't worry about completely covering the eyes, nose or mouth as these will be painted with black later.

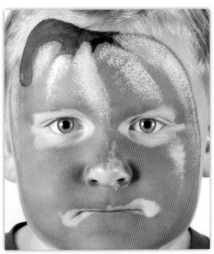

2 Use a no. 3 round brush and dark green to paint the pumpkin stem at the top of the forehead. Stipple yellow highlights under the stem with a sponge.

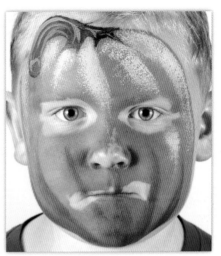

3 Highlight the stem with light green and a no. 3 round brush. Gently drag red onto the chin and cheeks with a sponge.

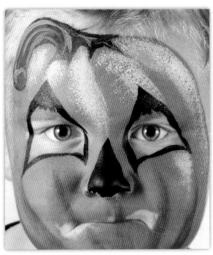

4 Paint a triangle shape onto the nose and outline the eyes with triangles using black and a no. 3 round brush.

5 Continue using the same brush and color to fill in the eyes and paint the mouth.

6 Outline the pumpkin face in black and outline the eyes, nose and mouth with yellow and a no. 3 round brush. Sponge white highlights into the stem and at the top of the pumpkin.

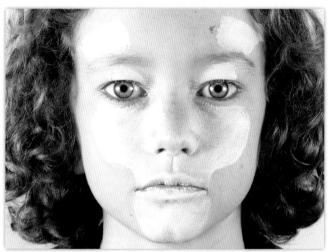

1 Sponge white onto the eyelids, above the eyebrows, along the sides of the nose, across the cheeks and over the mouth and chin. Make sure to leave the top of the nose blank.

2 Sponge horns onto the forehead and fill in the rest of the face with brown. Use the clean end of the sponge to feather the brown into the white, blending the line where the colors meet.

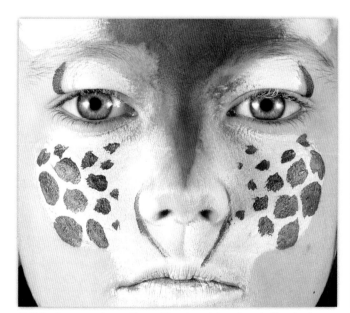

3 Using brown and a no. 3 round brush, paint spots onto the cheeks. Start with large spots on the outside, making them gradually smaller the closer they get toward the eyes. Outline the nose and eyelids in brown.

4 Continue using the no. 3 round brush to outline the face with black. Make the outline around the horn tips extra thick. Paint teardrop shapes for nostrils and black wing shapes for the inside of the ears.

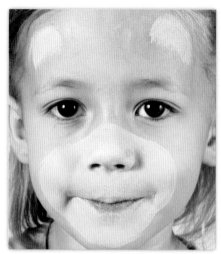

1 Sponge light tan/ivory around the mouth, nose and chin. Sponge two semicircle shapes onto the forehead with the same color.

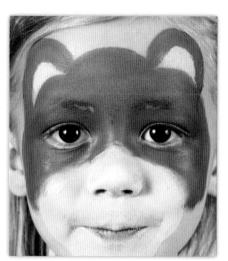

2 Sponge brown around the eyes and mask of the face, as well as around the semi-circle shapes to form the ears.

3 With black and a no. 3 round brush, paint the nose and outline the face. Drag your brushstrokes out along the light tan part of the ears to give them a furry look.

4 Continue using the same brush and color to paint a line running from the forehead to the bridge of the nose. Add some short horizontal lines across that for stitches. Paint eyelashes and another line running from the nose to the top lip. Touch up the brown and tan areas where needed and paint tan highlights at the top of the head and ears.

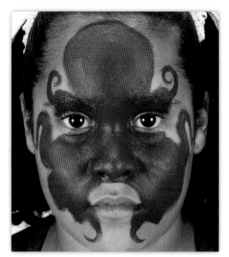

1 Sponge a basecoat of red onto the face in the basic shape of an octopus. Use a no. 3 round brush to pull out the tips of the tentacles.

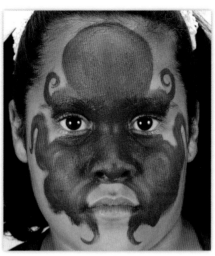

2 Sponge orange highlights on top of the head, eyebrows and tentacles.

3 With a no. 3 round brush, paint the bottoms of the tentacles pink. Begin painting scales in yellow. Continue using the no. 3 round brush for the remaining steps.

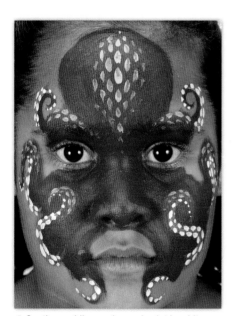

4 Continue adding scales and paint in white dots for the suction cups.

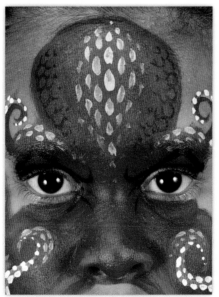

5 Paint scales on the sides of the head, add arched eyebrows, and line the eyelids with black.

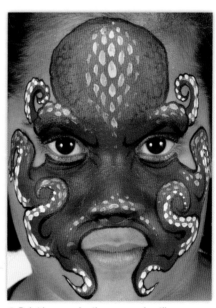

6 Paint bags under the eyes and outline the entire body in black, including the individual tentacles. Add some additional scales with yellow.

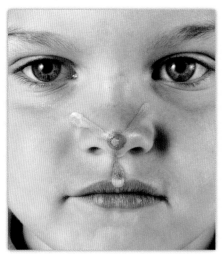

1 Use a no. 3 round brush to paint the plane's propeller on the center of the nose in gray. Continue using the no. 3 round brush for the remaining steps.

2 Paint a bullseye design around the propeller in black and white.

3 Paint the wings and fuselage of the plane in blue.

4 Use white to paint the cockpit and add detail to the wings. Outline the cockpit with black.

5 Paint the tail of the plane in dark blue. Use black to paint and detail the landing gear.

6 Outline the plane with black and finish adding details.

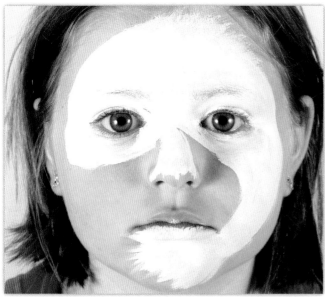

1 Sponge a basecoat of white onto the face in the basic shape of a koi.

2 Sponge turquoise along the koi's underbelly and tail to suggest water. Use a mix of red and orange to sponge a pattern onto the koi's body.

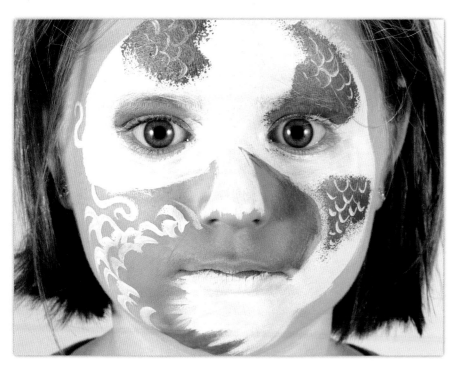

3 Use a sponge to shade in some blue above the eye and add a bit of blue into the water. With a no. 3 round brush and white, paint crests on the waves and scales on the red-orange areas of the body. Give the koi some whiskers as well. Continue with the no. 3 round brush for the remaining steps.

4 Outline the waves and koi's body and detail the fins with black.

5 Paint the koi's lips with the same red-orange mixture you used for the body pattern. Add some black scales in white areas of the koi's body to finish.

90

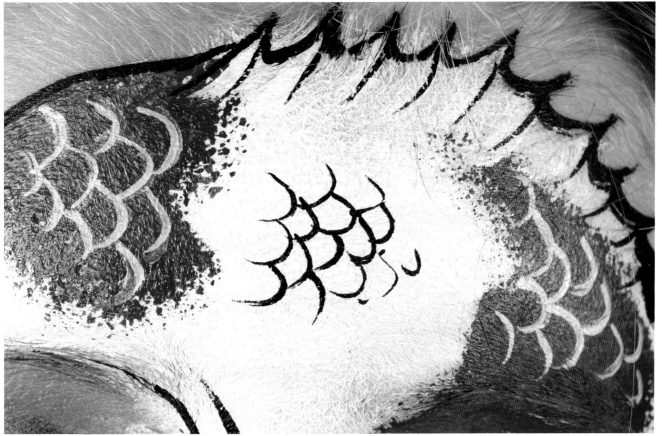

KEEP IT SIMPLE

Painting scales in small patches will help to create a look that is not too busy.

GET INSPIRED

The "hooks" in the wave crests were inspired by traditional Japanese artwork.

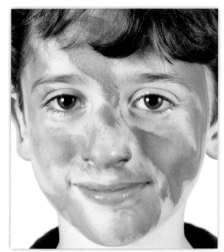

1 Mix a bit of brown with green to tone down the brightness of the color. Use a sponge to smear the mixture in random patterns across the face.

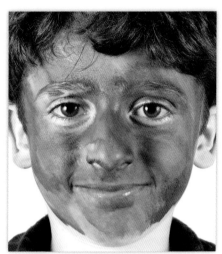

2 Sponge brown into the rest of the clear areas.

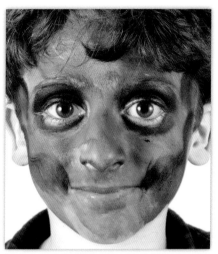

3 Sponge black around the eyes. Shadow the temples and under the cheekbones.

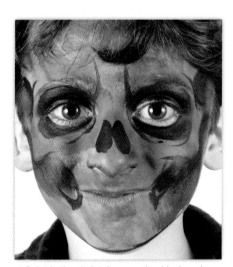

4 Paint in the skeletal nose using black and a no. 3 round brush. Paint black lines around the eyes and following the contours of the cheekbones. Continue using the no. 3 round brush for the remaining steps.

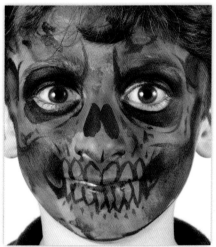

5 Paint the teeth. Use the side of the brush to make black smudges along the side of the face. This will help to heighten the camouflage effect.

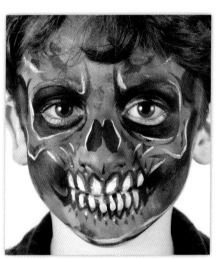

6 Fill in the teeth and outline the contours of the face with white.

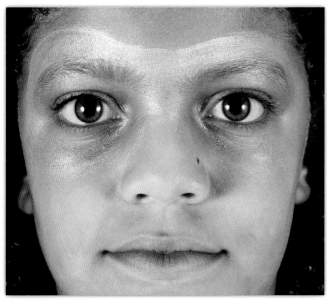

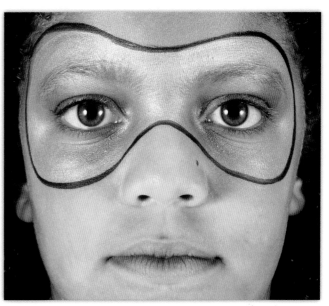

1 Sponge a gold basecoat around the eyes in the shape of a mask.

2 Lightly sponge purple onto the eyelids and pink under the eyebrows. Outline the mask with black and a no. 3 round brush. Continue using the no. 3 round brush for the remaining steps.

3 Paint cat's eyes shapes around the eyes and add diagonal lines across the mask in black.

4 Paint diagonal stripes running in the opposite direction from the first set of strips to create a crisscross pattern. Add black dots all along the edge of the mask.

5 Using the scalloping technique, paint around each dot lining the mask's edge. Place another dot on top of each scallop.

6 Paint white dots along the edge of the mask and on the points where the crisscrossed lines meet.

7 Highlight the top of the eyes with white. Add purple lipstick to finish.

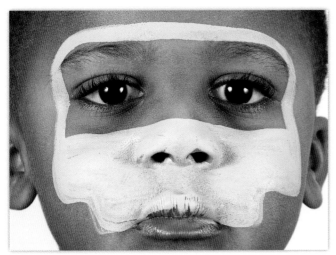

1 Paint the basic jeep shape onto the face in light blue with a no. 6 round brush.

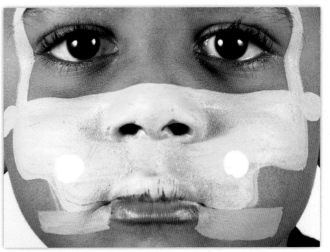

2 Switch to a no. 3 round brush and paint the bumper in gray and the headlights in white. Add side view mirrors in light blue. Continue using the no. 3 round brush for the remaining steps.

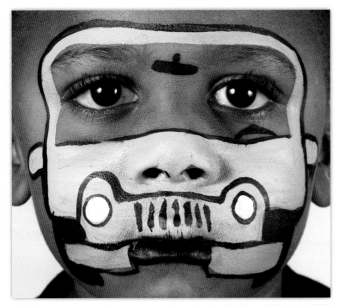

3 With black, paint in the grill and outline the headlights and bumper. Add tires, a steering wheel and a rearview mirror. Outline the body of the jeep.

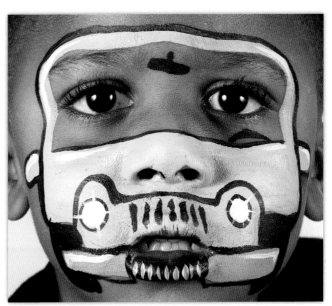

4 Paint white highlights over the whole jeep to finish.

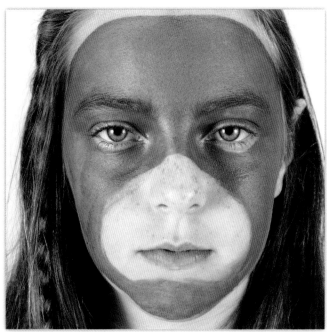

1 Mix neon pink with dark blue to get a bright purple color. Sponge a basecoat over the face, leaving the area around the nose and mouth clear.

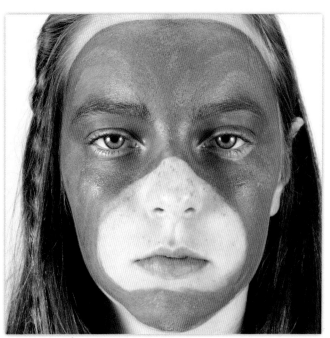

2 Stipple in neon pink highlights with a sponge.

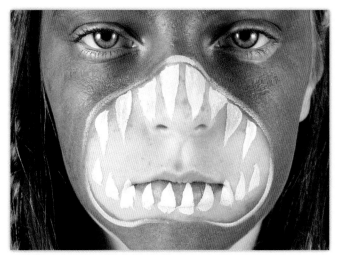

3 With a no. 3 round brush, paint a white outline around the edge of the clear area to define the monster's mouth, then paint the teeth.

4 Use red and a no. 3 round brush to paint the tongue, gums and areas under the eyes. Paint in white highlights on the forehead, chin and around the eyes. Sponge black shadows over the eyes.

5 Outline the teeth and fill in the mouth with black and a no. 3 round brush. Continue using the no. 3 round brush for the remaining steps.

6 Paint in the nose and add wrinkles around the eyes and mouth. Paint pink highlights on the gums and tongue.

7 Add more wrinkles on the forehead in black. Paint yellow "stains" onto the teeth and fleck the tongue and gums with white.

8 Use black to outline the face. Paint in black spots, making them larger on the outside and gradually smaller as you move in toward the center. Line the eyes with black to finish.

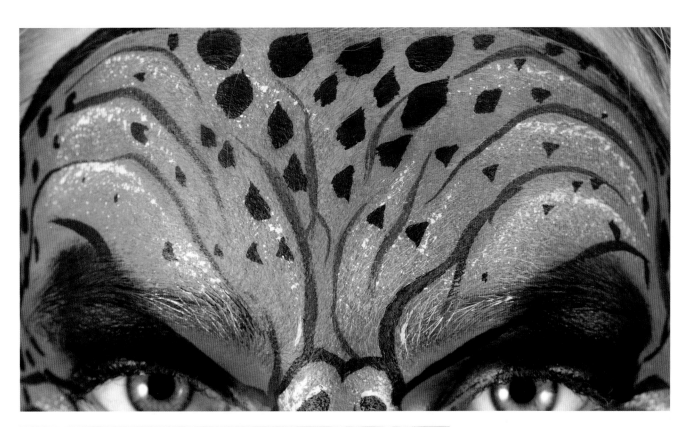

IT'S ALL IN THE DETAILS
The spots were done with the side of a round brush. Be sure to paint the inside of the nostrils to camouflage the nose.

103

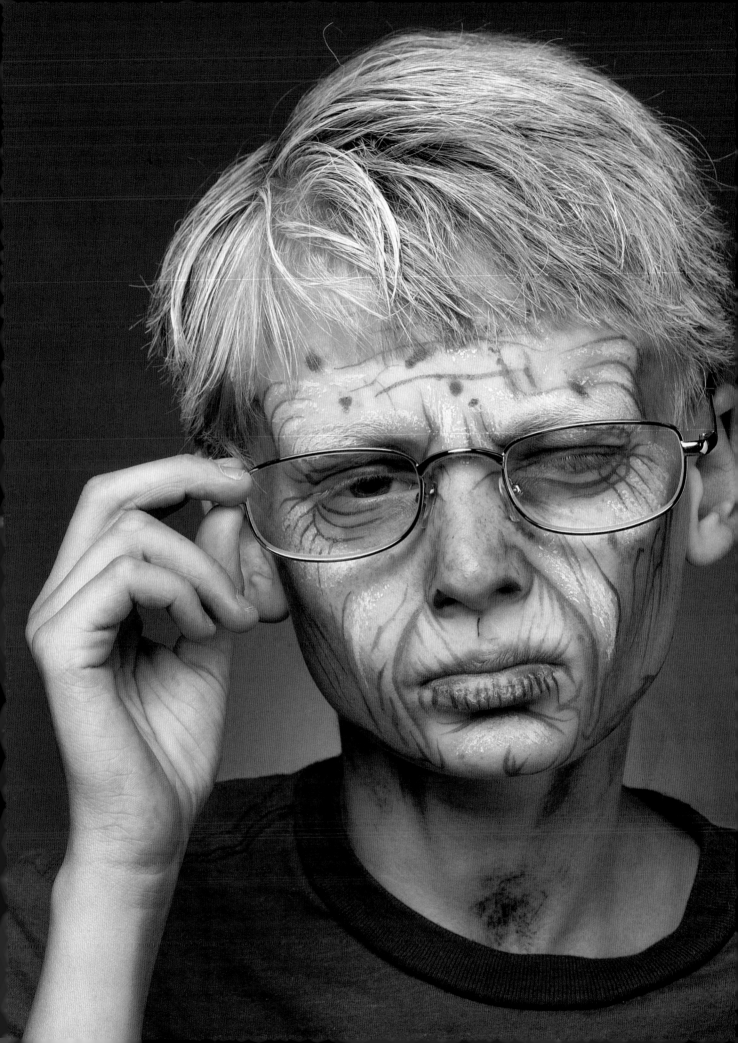

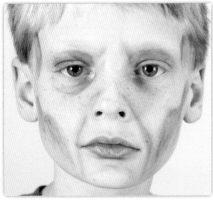

1 Mix brown and purple together to get a "brownple" shade. Use a sponge to lightly shade around the eyes, temples, cheekbones and laugh lines.

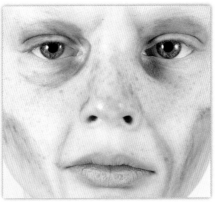

2 Sponge a light flesh color onto the lips. Water down a bit of red and sponge it over the nose.

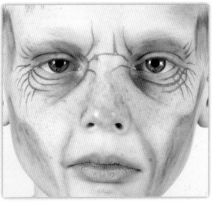

3 Use brown and a no. 3 round brush to paint in crow's feet and bags under the eyes.

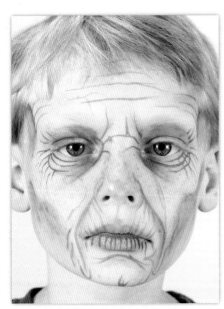

4 Paint wrinkles on the forehead and around the lips and chin with brown and a no. 3 round brush.

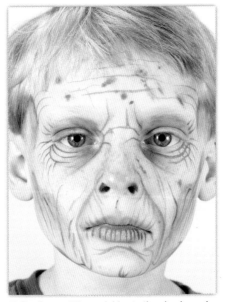

5 Continue adding wrinkles to the cheeks and jawline using the same brush and color. Mix a little bit of black with brown. Paint liver spots on the forehead by tapping the brush onto the skin and letting the color bleed out. Paint around the edges of the nostrils to give them a flared look.

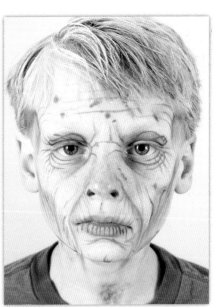

6 Mix a bit of the flesh color with white and stipple in highlights using a sponge. Add more wrinkles around the eyelids to define them. Brush a bit of white paint into the hair to complete the look.

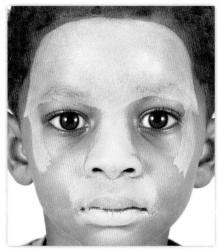

1 Sponge a lime-green basecoat onto the face in the shape of a turtle.

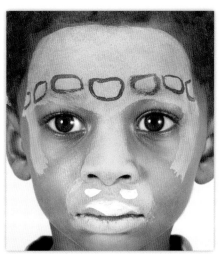

2 Use white and a no. 3 round brush to paint half-circle shapes for the turtle's eyes. Highlight the upper lip with white. With brown, paint loose rectangle shapes onto the forehead to form the rim of the shell.

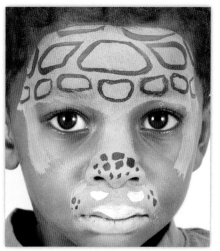

3 Continue using the same brush and color to finish adding rectangle shapes to the shell and paint spots on the turtle's face.

4 Use a filbert brush to drag the brown inward from the rectangle edges. Add brown spots on the arms with a no. 3 round brush. Continue using the no. 3 round brush for the remaining steps.

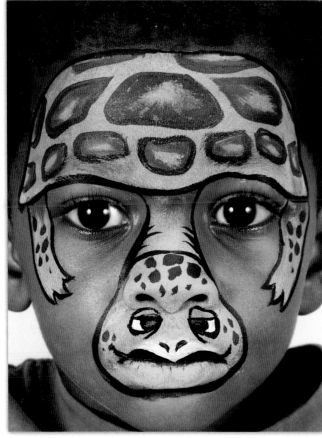

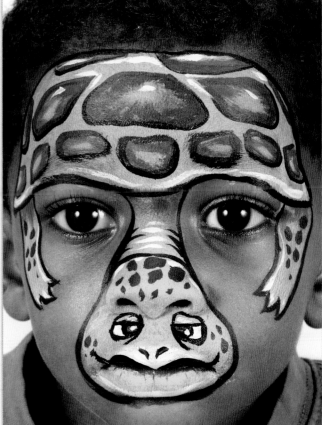

5 Paint the turtle's eyes, nostrils and mouth, define the neck, and outline the entire body in black.

6 Paint black shadows under the shell shapes. Highlight with white all around.

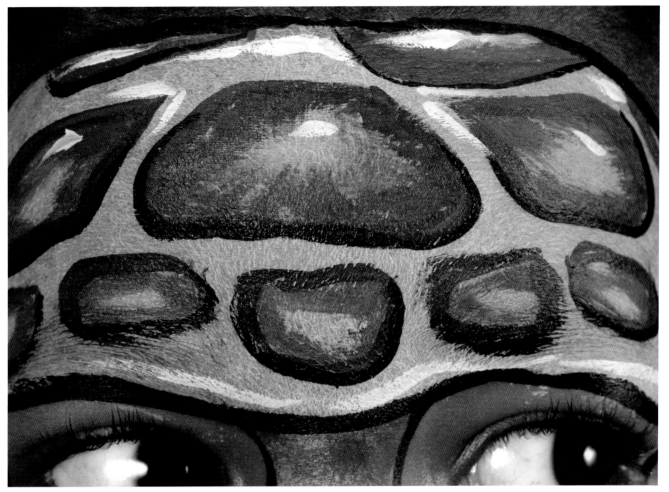

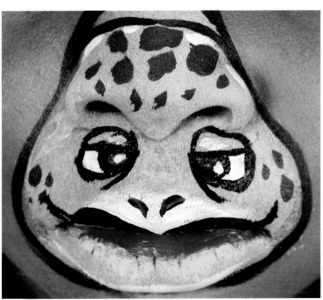

OUTLINE, DRAG AND UNDERLINE

When painting the scales on the shell, outline with a thick stroke then use a dry brush to drag the brown paint inward. Finish by underlining the shapes with black.

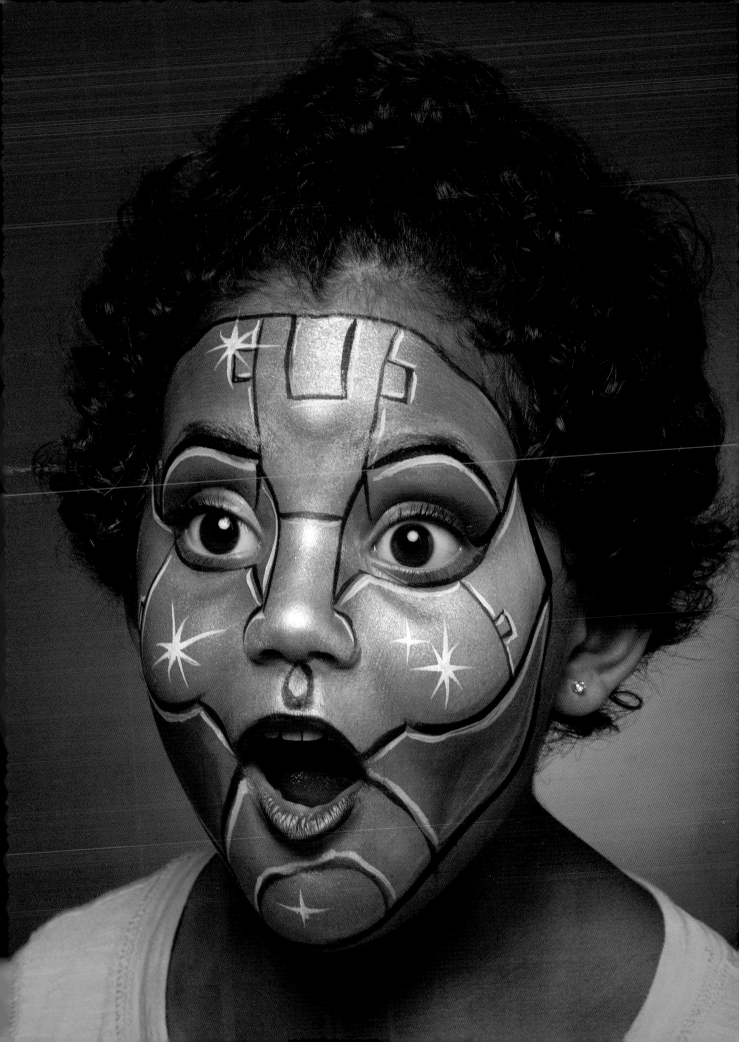

1 Sponge a gold metallic basecoat over the entire face.

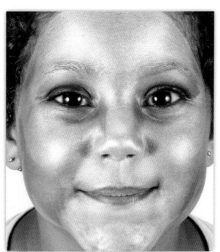

2 Use a sponge to shade the cheeks and nose with brown. Shade above the eyes with black.

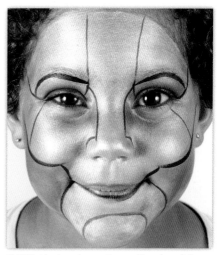

3 With black and a no. 3 round brush, paint in eyebrows and several lines following the contours of the facial anatomy.

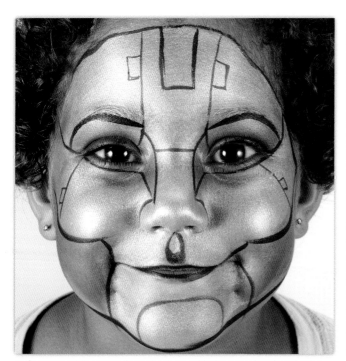

4 Continue adding more lines and rivets with the same brush and color.

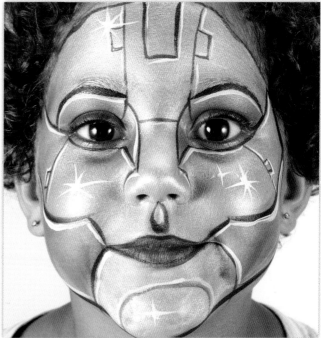

5 Add white highlights along the black lines and paint stars onto the forehead, cheeks and chin with a no. 3 round brush.

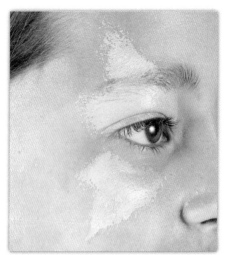

1 Sponge yellow wing shapes from the corner of the eye at a 45 degree angle. Stipple with a clean sponge to break up the smooth texture a bit.

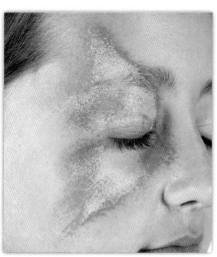

2 Use the tip of a sponge to stipple orange around the yellow.

3 Paint a red flame pattern over the wing using a no. 3 round brush.

4 Continuing with the same brush and color, paint the fairy along the side of the nose.

5 Use neon orange and a no. 3 round brush to highlight the fairy and fill in any empty spots in the flames.

6 With a sponge, stipple in some yellow around the flames to suggest fly-away embers. Highlight with white. Paint yellow, orange and red above the opposite eye to balance things out. Tie it all together with red lipstick.

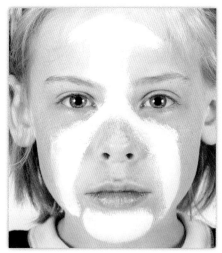

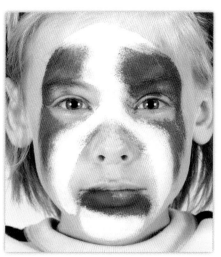

1 Sponge a basecoat of white onto the center of the forehead, running down bridge of the nose, inner cheeks, and across the chin.

2 Sponge brown around the eyes, outer cheeks and chin. Bounce the clean back of the sponge along the areas where the brown and white meet to loosely blend the colors.

3 Sponge black under the eyes and onto the eyelids, nose and area around the mouth. Use the sponge create the bulldog's ears at the top of the forehead as well.

4 Use a no. 3 round brush to paint gums onto the mouth in pink. Paint the teeth and highlight the ears and nose with white.

5 Outline the face and teeth and add bags under the eyes using black and a no. 3 round brush. Add some tiny white dots along the gums to make him look slobbery.

1 Sponge white onto the side of the face, temple and forehead in the rough shape of a horse.

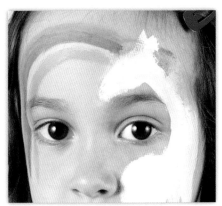

2 Use a sponge to drag bands of pink, orange, yellow and green across the forehead to begin the rainbow. Sponge orange, yellow and green behind the unicorn's ears to begin the mane.

3 Still using the sponge, drag blue and purple across the forehead to complete the rainbow. Finish the mane off with some purple and blue as well. Sponge in purple and pink clouds at the end of the rainbow and covering the unicorn's feet.

4 Paint the unicorn's face and horn, detail the mane, and outline the body with black and a no. 3 round brush.

5 Still using the no. 3 round brush, paint in a rainbow tail. With white, add spirals to the horn, paint stars across the rainbow and highlight the clouds. Tie it together with purple lipstick.

DOWNLOAD A FREE BONUS DEMO AT **IMPACT-BOOKS.COM/WOLFEBROTHERS**

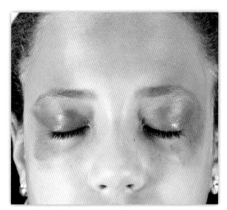

1 Sponge light green above the eyebrows and light blue under the eyebrows and on the temples. Mix pink and blue to get a light purple, and sponge this on the eyelids and under the corners of the eyes.

2 Use a no. 3 round brush and black to paint three swirls on each side radiating out from the corners of the eyes. While painting, alternate back and forth between sides to maintain symmetry. Continue using a no. 3 round brush for the remaining steps.

3 Paint more black swirls extending off the original swirls. Add teardrop shapes at the corners of the eyes in descending size.

4 Continue building up black teardrops under the eyes and along the swirls in descending size.

5 Paint white scallops and teardrops at the ends of the black teardrops to add highlights. Tie it all together with some light purple lipstick.

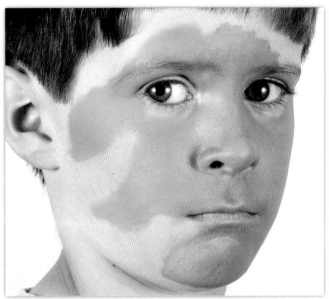

1 Sponge a green basecoat in the shape of a T-Rex's profile onto the face.

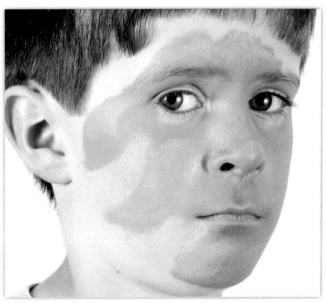

2 Sponge yellow highlights into the areas that form the T-Rex's head, mouth and shoulder.

3 Use dark green and a no. 3 round brush to add stripes on the head and scales on the bottom jaw. Paint a dark green ridge above the eye and paint in the T-Rex's hand. Continue with the no. 3 round brush for the remaining steps.

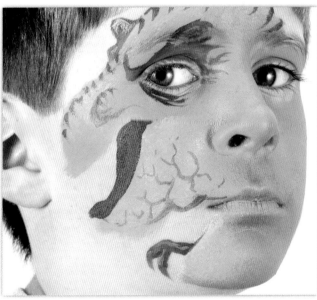

4 Paint a bit of red under the eye and paint in the tongue. Add yellow highlights to the arm and on the opposite side of the face.

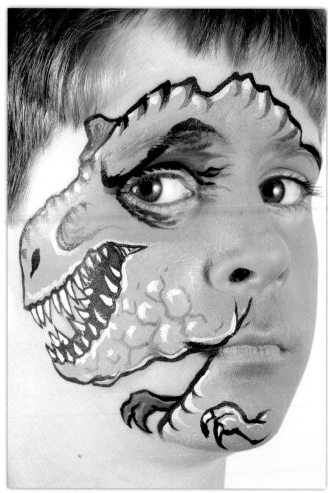

5 Paint white teardrop shapes along the mouth to form the teeth. Highlight the scales with white.

6 Outline everything in black. Continue using black to paint the second arm. Use white to paint the claws on the second arm and add highlights.

HIGHLIGHTS CREATE THE ILLUSION OF DEPTH

Highlighting the edge of the mouth will help make the inside of the mouth look deeper.

USE TONE TO SUGGEST DISTANCE

Paint the far hand in a darker tone than the near hand. This will make it look more distant.

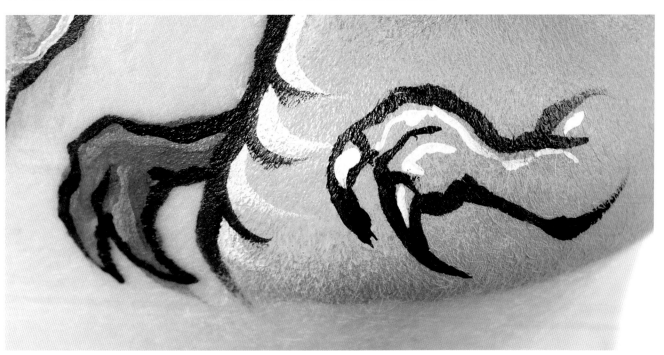

Index

Dedication

Nick and Brian would like to dedicate this book to you.

Acknowledgments

Brian would like to thank love, light, God and his wife, Dara for taking care of him and being there. Thanks also to Trinity and the rest of the family, including our friends and peers.

Nick would like to thank Brian, his better half.

FUN **FACE PAINTING IDEAS** FOR KIDS. Copyright © 2013 by Nick and Brian Wolfe. Manufactured in China. All rights reserved. No part of this book may be reproduced in any form or by any electronic or mechanical means including information storage and retrieval systems without permission in writing from the publisher, except by a reviewer who may quote brief passages in a review. Published by IMPACT Books, an imprint of F+W Media, Inc., 10151 Carver Road, Suite 200, Blue Ash, Ohio, 45242. (800) 289-0963. First Edition.

Other fine IMPACT Books are available from your favorite bookstore, art supply store or online supplier. Visit our website at **fwmedia.com**.

17   16   15   14   13   5   4   3   2   1

Distributed in Canada by Fraser Direct
100 Armstrong Avenue
Georgetown, ON, Canada L7G 5S4
Tel: (905) 877-4411

Distributed in the U.K. and Europe
by F&W Media International, LTD
Brunel House, Forde Close, Newton Abbot,
TQ12 4PU, UK
Tel. (+44) 1626 323200, Fax: (+44) 1626 323319
Email: enquiries@fwmedia.com

Distributed in Australia by Capricorn Link
P.O. Box 704, S. Windsor NSW, 2756 Australia
Tel: (02) 4560-1600, Fax: (02) 4577-5288
Email: books@capricornlink.com.au

EDITED BY **CHRISTINA RICHARDS**
DESIGNED BY **JENNIFER HOFFMAN**
PRODUCTION COORDINATED BY **MARK GRIFFIN**
PHOTOGRAPHY BY **AL PARRISH** AND **CHRISTINE POLOMSKY**

Metric Conversion Chart

TO CONVERT	TO	MULTIPLY BY
Inches	Centimeters	2.54
Centimeters	Inches	0.4
Feet	Centimeters	30.5
Centimeters	Feet	0.03
Yards	Meters	0.9
Meters	Yards	1.1

ABOUT THE AUTHORS

Award-winning, world-renowned artists/instructors **Brian and Nick Wolfe** are known for their fast-paced face and body art techniques. They began their careers at Universal Studios Florida working for the prosthetics department and Enjoy Your Face Inc., painting the guests' faces in the park. After contributing to face-painting publications, teaching classes and attending conventions, the twins were offered an endorsement deal with a marketing and development company, and Wolfe Brothers Face Art & FX was born. Nick and Brian worked with them for four years, flying around the world, sharing their techniques and products. They have previously published ten step-by-step "cheat" books, as well as *Extreme Face Painting* (IMPACT Books, 2010).

Now they are traveling and teaching the joy of body art to the rest of the planet. They regularly participate in the Face & Body Art International Convention, and in workshops at trade shows and makeup schools, sharing their all-time favorite monster and dragon faces. They won first place for the World Bodypainting Award Championship in Seeboden, Austria in 2009. Brian also won first place in the brush and sponge category for face painting at the 2011 World Bodypainting Festival in Portschach, Austria. Visit their website at eviltwinfx.com.

Ideas. Instruction. Inspiration.

Download FREE bonus demos at **impact-books.com/wolfebrothers**.

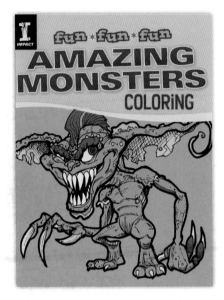

Check out these *IMPACT* titles at impact-books.com!

These and other fine **IMPACT** products are available at your local art & craft retailer, bookstore or online supplier. Visit our website at **impact-books.com**.

Follow **IMPACT** for the latest news, free wallpapers, free demos and chances to win **FREE BOOKS**!

IMPACT-BOOKS.COM

- Connect with your favorite artists
- Get the latest in comic, fantasy and sci-fi art instruction, tips and techniques
- Be the first to get special deals on the products you need to improve your art